Welcome to the RCI
Points Bible
2019 Edition

Welcome to the RCI Points Bible
Bible
2019 Edition

Welcome to the RCI Points Bible
2019 Edition

RCI POINTS BIBLE

TIPS, TRICKS, AND MORE SECRETS

Printed in the United States
10987654321

FOREWARD

Welcome to the "RCI Points Bible - 2019 User Guide", the newest version of the "RCI Points User Guide – Tip, Tricks and Secrets".

This manual will become an indispensable part of your current and future travel plans. Inside you will find many valuable Tips, Tricks and Secrets. Among these precious nuggets of gold, you will find out how to get multiple weeks of vacation time for just one week of ownership.

Another secret that will be revealed is how to make reservations at luxury resorts (The Registry Collection). Many RCI Points owners aren't aware of this unrivaled collection of ultimate vacation experiences.

The "Registry Collection" is an offering of upscale resorts that have the highest rated accommodations in the world located in incredibly beautiful locations. And just think, you can use your RCI Points and RCI Points Membership to vacation in pure luxury.

This latest version of the RCI Points User Guide also has a section that contains dramatic new information contained 2018 RCI Press Releases. This timely information will give purchasers of this book up to date information on what's new at RCI. You will find included in this guide updates on the new resorts that have just been added and made available to RCI Points Owners and members.

The press releases outline the addition of over 200 new locations including many vacation resort locations in Japan and Asia.. As new press releases are published, they will be added to the book, and published on a blog site.

If you are an RCI Point's owner, or are considering becoming one, you will find this User guide to be of inestimable value!

Several years ago, I wrote and published "RCI Points User Guide – Tips, Tricks and Secrets". Since the initial publication date, thousands of copies have sold. This guide is now outdated and is being taken off the market. It has been replaced with this new and updated edition.

The original RCI Points User Guide was written as a result of comments made by many RCI Points owners. The general consensus was that it was challenging when it came to making reservations with their points.

The bottom line at that time was that RCI Point System was certainly a great program, and there were 1000's of vacation destinations available to owners.

However, there was little actual value with their investment if RCI owners couldn't successfully make travel reservations. Their investment was worthless if they were unable to use their points. There was a major need for an RCI point's Owner's Manual.

The author had worked at several RCI affiliate resorts as a front-line marketing representative. He made it a point (excuse the play on words) to learn everything the he could about the RCI Points System.

It seemed logical to the author of the original user guide that an easy to use and informative portable book would provide solutions to the challenging dilemma that RCI Point's owners were faced with.

The original user guide was easy to read, easy to use, and easy to understand. A successful RCI Point's book evolved. The writer listened to users and owners and developed chapters in the original book that would directly address confusing issues while making it easy to make successful vacation reservations.

Many positive comments have been received through the years. As a result of reader feedback, new chapters and valuable information have been added to this updated version.

You will find in the following chapters new information, new solutions new benefits of the RCI Points System, and money saving tips.

RCI has added many new resorts to their system. You will be shown how to access these and how to make reservations at several somewhat secretive and exclusive luxury resorts.

This book will let you in on the many secrets and will enlighten you with many little known facts. Read on....

...and many Happy Trails!

Inspiring Travel Quotes

"And then there is the most dangerous risk of all — the risk of spending your life not doing what you want on the bet you can buy yourself the freedom to do it later."
Anonymous

"Travel is fatal to prejudice, bigotry, and narrow mindedness."
Mark Twain.

Travel makes one modest. You see what a tiny place you occupy in the world." - Gustav Flaubert.

" I'm in love with cities I've never been to and people I've never met."
John Green.

"Don't listen to what they say. Go see."
Anonymous

" **Take only memories, leave only footprints.**"
Chief Seattle.

"Travel is not a destination; it is just a new way of seeing things."

"Life is either a daring adventure, or it is nothing at all".
Helen Keller

"Dare to live the life you've always wanted. Because in the end, you won't remember the time you spent working in the office or mowing your lawn. Climb that goddamn mountain!"
Jack Kerouac

"Jobs fill your pockets, but adventures fill your soul".
Jamie Lyn Beatty

"To Travel is to Live" –
Hans Christian Andersen

The following logos and registered trademarks of Resorts Condominiums International (RCI) are used in this book.

RCI®
RCI Points®
RCI Last CallSM
RCI PlatinumSM
RCI Cruise PerksSM
RCI Shopping PerksSM
RCI Extra VacationsSM Getaways

RCI Points Bible

———————

Printed in USA
10987654321

Dedication

To "Auntie Norm" – thank you for everything.
There are no words…

Table of Contents

ACKNOWLEDGMENT

To the millions of happy Timeshare   users and

15

travelers. Thank you for your input and your valuable sharing in person and on various internet sites. Your wisdom has been most helpful. Blessings to you!

CHAPTER ONE

BRIEF HISTORIES
OF
RCI AND THE TIMESHARE INDUSTRY

This is introductory information about the history of RCI and background on the beginning and evolution of the Timeshare industry. Here is information that might help you build a foundation that will enhance your vacation happiness in the future. With this knowledge, you will feel more comfortable and confident using points.

This brief history of RCI and Timeshare will be very helpful in briefing you on how the Timeshare industry and the RCI Point's System can benefit your travel and vacation experiences. It will also provide insights as how everything came about in the RCI Point's world. It is an interesting, if not valuable story that will at least enlighten you.

They say that knowledge is power and knowledge of the history and evolution of Timeshare will help you understand today's concepts and terminology much better. As a fellow RCI Points Timeshare owner, at one time the author had also been curious as to how all of this started and evolved.

Who thought up the initial concept of Timeshare as we know it today? Another question that intrigues me is - where in the world were the first Timeshares, Fractionals or shared Intervals sold?

Was it a well-planned enterprise or a happenstance set of random events and circumstances?

The origins of Timeshare can be traced back to Europe in the 1960's. There were some exciting and interesting things happening around the world in that timeframe.

It was a time of considerable growth and development for the tourism industry worldwide because of the exploding growth of commercial air travel. Timeshare sales were helped considerably by this change in lifestyle.

Several sources indicate that the Timeshare industry began in Switzerland in a small town called Baar sometime around 1963. There were three men who were instrumental in developing the concept and they eventually became the founders of Happimag, a vacation or holiday company.

They came up with the idea that vacationers should own their vacations instead of renting them. Who knows, perhaps the term "Vacation Ownership" came out of their initial ideas.

People had a strong desire to have a guaranteed week at their favorite resort every year during ski season.

Early innovators explained to these people that it was much less expensive for several families to jointly own weeks at a chalet and to take turns using it rather than incur the considerable cash outlay of building an expensive ski lodge for each family.

A French company began offering its Timeshare product in the 1964-1968 timeframe. The initial resort offered by this company was a ski lodge based in the French Alps. This vacation/ski spot was called SuperDevoluy. Interested fractional buyers were drawn to Doumier's advertising slogan, **"No need to rent the room; buy the hotel, it's cheaper!"**

This company that is known for initiating the Timeshare concept was called Hapimag and was based in Baar, Switzerland. Shortly after founding the company in September of 1963, Hapimag's owners began buying up resort properties in Italy, Spain, and Switzerland.

Hapimag offered its members an extensive resort selection on a right-to-use basis instead of deeded ownership.

Right to use did not offer owners any form of a real estate deed or in other words – they didn't have true ownership of a property. Hapimag is still in operation today and they are a large independent exchange company in Europe.

Skiers and vacationers liked the idea and sales took off. During ski season, they had a guarantee of staying at the ski resort where they usually purchased one or more weeks of usage every year. The concept was also very timely, because there was a worldwide glut of condominiums at this time.

People involved in the Timeshare industry took advantage of this excess inventory and converted the condo complexes to Timeshare units. Both the Timeshare industry and the developers sitting on unsold inventory of condos obviously benefited.

Timeshare entrepreneurs had immediate access to 1000's of condos around the world that developers were trying to liquidate. Just like that – a large and thriving industry was born.

So much for Europe – but how did the Timeshare concept get started in the United States? In the US, timesharing per se was first available in Hawaii beginning in 1969. Kauai Kailani on the island Kauai was the initial condominium destination to offer Americans a Timeshare program.

Florida was the first state offering Timesharing in the continental US in the early 1970s. Florida was poised for the Timeshare concept and it was instrumental in introducing the Timeshare concept in the southeast.

A California company called Innisfree was the first in the US to offer deeded ownership Timeshares. Their first development was at Lake Tahoe and it was here that the word "Timeshare" was first commonly used in the US.

Several Timeshare developers came up with the name "Timeshare" after observing groups of people sharing time – or timesharing on computers. Thus, the name Timeshare originally came from the computer world and the term would ultimately become a household word. All of the pieces were in place and starting in 1974 Timeshare ownership grew at breakneck speed.

A problem for early Timeshare owners existed in the fact that they had no way of swapping or exchanging their condo with other like-minded condo owners in other geographical areas.

Owners wanted to trade to go to different places other than where they owned. Several small and ineffective exchange companies gradually popped up in an attempt address this need.

Owners would place (deposit) their condo or Timeshare with these exchange companies hoping that the exchange company could find someone at another geographic location that wanted to exchange for their unit.

To make this work, you needed 1000's of people that wanted to make an exchange.

Unfortunately, this normally wasn't the case and there weren't enough registered Timeshare owners with the exchange companies to make it work.

In 1974 RCI appeared on the scene and they had the missing pieces to the puzzle. RCI had an effective exchange system that would eventually handle thousands or even millions of exchanges.

RCI was started by Jon and Crystal De Haan. They had a great idea and their timing couldn't have been better. The De Haans and their business called RCI (Resorts Condominiums International) had an interesting and unique beginning.

In the mid 70's, developers who had overbuilt during the condominium boom were looking for an effective, quick, and profitable way to sell or generate income from their empty condos.

As a result of the Timeshare explosion, many of these developers or builders converted their apartment inventory to Timeshares as the Timeshare concept had become very viable. In the beginning the De Hanns started a small business that made it possible for condo owners to easily exchange with each other.

These weren't Timeshare resorts as we know them today, but condos with fractional ownership. At this same time many developers were using Timeshare to liquidate their unsold condos. The De Haan's exchange approach was perfect for the budding Timeshare industry. As mentioned earlier, the condo and construction industry was providing inventory to meet owner demand.

This incredibly new business direction was started almost by accident. The De Haan's exchange concept allowed people who had purchased one or two weeks of Timeshare to exchange with like-minded owners of Timeshare units in other geographical locations.

Timeshare owners loved the convenience of exchanging for other locations around the world. Unlike the computers used at RCI today, they originally used index cards to keep track of 100's and 1000's of exchanges for members.

The need for this type of exchange service gave

their business a huge boost and RCI was on the way towards becoming a large, effective and well respected company.

By the time that the early 1990's rolled around, there were over four million Timeshare owners worldwide. These owners usually owned deeded property at some 2,300 time-sharing facilities at different geographical locations.

At about this same time, several major hotel chains saw the potential of vacation timesharing and they wanted to start expanding into this business. Marriott was the first followed by Sheraton, Ramada, Hilton, Disney, Four Seasons, Radisson, and Hyatt.

Many industry observers believe that RCI was responsible for the real introduction and growth of Timeshare around the world. Today there are over 7000 Timeshare developments in over 100 countries. People enjoy going to new and exciting destinations that were financially out of reach for them in the past.

The US accounts for roughly 45% of all Timeshares in the world. Approximately 1600 Timeshare resorts are located in the United States and this is currently more than any other country.

Timeshare travelers come from 270 countries. Today, Timeshare vacations are a way of life for millions of people. To them, traveling to exotic and beautiful places is no longer just a dream – the Timeshare concept provides an inexpensive and easy to use way to see the world.

CHAPTER TWO

RCI POINTS? REMOVING THE MYSTERY

AN INTRODUCTION TO RCI POINTS

In the 1999 to 2001 timeframe, RCI launched their globally based points program. The introduction of this innovative vacation concept hit the Timeshare and Travel Industry like an atomic bomb.

Within a few years over 1 million people were using this new RCI Points System to enhance their travel and vacation plans. Companies like Marriott and Wyndham were quick to copy with their versions of this new travel concept.

What is so exciting and appealing about the RCI Points System?

Up until this travel revolution, vacationing by Timeshare exchange had many challenges and major problems. An owner was severely limited in his ability to exchange his Timeshare. He usually couldn't trade up (even if he owned multiple condos). He also couldn't see the availability of units that had better trading power than his condo, even if he owned multiple condos with strong combined trading power.

Owners were blocked from looking at more attractive condos. If they had a three-bedroom unit and exchanged for a one bedroom, guess what. Tough luck. There was no way of compensating the owner for his lost trading power.

This limited way of trading or exchanging was very unfair in most circumstances. Many owners complained about this flawed form of trading. Mysterious resort rankings didn't allow them the flexibility to accommodate their individual vacationing wants and needs.

RCI Points to the rescue. The fundamental concept of the RCI Points System is quite straight forward. Every condo or unit in the RCI affiliate resort listing was assigned a point value. Points were a form of vacation currency. Points were treated like travel money and points could be used for many things besides resort usage. It was like having a vacation savings account.

Points could be used for non-accommodation things such as air fare, car rentals, cruses, hotels, spas, green fees, entertainment venues and much more!

As with home ownership, every condo or "unit" in the RCI affiliate system has a different value, and it follows that each unit or condo will have a different point value. You might be wondering how these values are determined.

Here's how it works. The RCI Points value for a condo or villa is determined based upon several factors These factors include: supply and demand at that resort location, type of unit, number of bedrooms, ownership season, amenities, and evaluations from members who have previously stayed at this resort destination.

Your RCI Points are then debited to your account every year, on the first day of your "Use Year". Just in case your "Use Year" was never explained to you, here's a quick review. Technically, you became an RCI member the day the paper work was completed giving you the right of ownership to your condo or villa. However, Your use year begins on the first day of the following month for logistical reasons.

In the previous way of exchanging, if you didn't use your unit in any given year, too bad. You lost whatever trading or exchanging power your condo might have had. It was more than a 100% loss, as you still had to pay the maintenance fee.

With points, all or part of your points can be rolled over to the next use year if you don't use all or any part of your points in the current year. WOW. That's pretty cool! What an improvement! And in some cases, you can even roll your points over into the 3rd and 4th years!

And if you didn't have enough points to stay at your desired vacation destination when you wanted to, guess what? You could now borrow points from the next year in order to complete your reservation. Or, you didn't have to borrow from your future travel plans. You could even rent points in order to complete your vacation plans. The ultimate in flexibility.

In the old and antiquated "weeks" trading program you had to stay a week at a time, no short term or getaway vacations. With points, you can book vacations or getaways for shorter than a week. How about a weekend work break at a beautiful resort for 2 or 3 days? With points, reservations for 2, 3, 4 or 5 days can happen. You now didn't have to burn a whole week in exchange for a brief getaway.

With RCI Points, the world was now your oyster. You could stay at over 4000 resorts worldwide. Your dream vacation became a real possibility.

Through the years, RCI has continually improved

the Points System. They have added Platinum Points, Points Partners, hundreds of new resort locations, The Registry Collection (Luxury Resorts), and other enhancements to further heighten the flexibility of RCI Points membership and to give you the ultimate travel experience.

Additional information on the RCI Points System and how to get multiple weeks of vacation for one week of ownership will be explained in further chapters.

CHAPTER THREE

MAKING RESERVATIONS

TIPS, TRICKS & SECRETS

Making an RCI Points Reservation

Here is a brief overview of the RCI rules governing when and how you can make certain types of reservations. This is very important! Don't take a chance and try to make your critical vacation reservation outside of a reservation window. What is a an RCI "Reservation Window"? By understanding how Reservation Windows work, you will know when best to exchange. This means more available vacation options, more reservation flexibility, and happier vacation experiences!

A Reservation Window is essentially a window of opportunity where you can request a specific type of reservation with less competition from other RCI Subscribing Members. Each type of reservation at RCI affiliated resorts has a unique Reservation Window.

You always have an opportunity to book your Home Week before it is made available to other members. There are also Reservation Windows during which you have priority over available units at your Home Resort and at other resorts within your Home Group of resorts.

RCI Reservation at a weeks resort.

You want to choose from any of the available RCI Weeks affiliated resorts.

Reservation Window – is 2 years or less before check-in date.

You own fixed time and want to reserve the specific week and unit you own.

13-12 Months before your check-in date.

HOME RESORT - You own fixed or floating time, and want to reserve a unit at your Home Resort other than the one you own.

12-11 months before check-in date.

HOME GROUP

You want to reserve a unit at a resort which is part of a larger group of properties in your Home Group of resorts.

11-10 Months - before check-in date

STANDARD RESERVATION

You want to choose from any of the other available RCI Points affiliated resorts.

10 Months before check-in date

Important: Please note! – The Home Week, Home Resort and RCI Weeks Reservation Windows require seven-night stays.

During the Home Group and Standard Reservation Windows, reservations can be made for less than seven-nights.

By understanding how Reservation Windows work, you will know when best to exchange. This means more available vacation options, more reservation flexibility, and happier vacation experiences!

To START - Click on - Making a Standard Reservation online

Then follow the steps shown below when making any type of reservation:
Start by clicking on the 'RCI Points Vacation or Holidays' tab.

Click on standard reservation – and enter your dates and destinations. **Now click Continue.**

For information on any of the resorts displayed, **click on the resort name.** To view available units for any resorts, **click on Available Units.**

Select the unit that you'd like to reserve and **click Confirm**.

To complete your online booking, enter your payment details.

Now click Continue.

Verify your details and, if everything is correct, click Continue.

If you need to change anything, you can modify your details by **clicking on the Modify link.**

Your reservation - is now confirmed.

Making a home resort reservation on line

Click on Home Resort and input your **check-in date at the top of the page.**

The Home View - Available Units Resorts available to you will be displayed. Select the resort you wish to reserve and click continue.

Select which unit you wish to reserve and click Confirm.

Finally, verify all the details are correct and **click on continue to confirm your reservation.**

Enter your payment details. You can also select whether you'd like to add a Guest Certificate.

Hit Continue to confirm your reservation.

Here is another version of making points reservations.
Here the reservation process is outlined in a little more detail.

. After signing in, Click on the Search for an Exchange Tab at the top of the screen.

On the left side of the screen, you will see a column with the heading: **Select Filter From List.**

You will also see a map of the world to the right of this column. You can make a reservation in two ways, either with the filter or by **clicking on desired locations on the map. Click on the list view filter. Click on your desired location.**

After you click on your desired location - it will display the number of **resorts available.**

You can click on any resort.

At this point, a screen will come up with several pictures of the resort and it's amenities.

Click on the green Available Units box.

You will now see three monthly calendars. with available check in dates in dark green.

Click on the upper right side of the calendar on the right (it will have a right arrow). Keep clicking until you come to the month you are looking for.

You should now be looking at orange boxes that say select unit, with the unit sizes above the box. Click on the Select Unit box for the size you desire

The next screen will show an I acknowledge ...... box. Click on that box if you want to confirm a reservation.
Below that box you will see Cancel, Confirm and Hold**. If you want to go ahead with the reservation**, click on either hold or confirm. Hold will hold the reservation for 24 hours and confirm will lock in the reservation.

The next screens are regarding payment and points

that will be subtracted from your account for this reservation.

Congratulations – you have used points to make a reservation in the RCI Point's System!

Important: The next thing to keep in mind is that you can make a reservation at a week's resort 2 days to 24 months in advance. You can only make a reservation at a point's resort 10 months out.

Here are the nightly fees that apply - between Sunday and Thursday:

- $49 for one night.
- $69 for two nights.
- $89 for three nights.
- $109 for four nights.
- $129 for five nights
- $139 for six nights
- $149 for seven nights

- Points required between Sunday and Thursday night: 1/12th of the required weekly points value (see RCI ultimate vacation guide to get weekly value).
- Points required for Friday and Saturday nights are 20% of the weekly value per night.

Remember, you can go to most week's resorts using the instant exchange approach. This means that

Stallion Springs in Southern California with Instant Exchange is 9,000 points instead of over 50,000 points outside of the last call window.

OK. Here is a mystery that needs to be solved before you can make non-instant exchange reservations at a <u>week's resort.</u>

Unlike point's resorts, weeks resorts in your RCI points catalog don't have points values on the RCI page where the resort is. How do you determine the required point value of a week's resort? Let's assume that I need to figure the required point value for one week at a week's resort in Arizona.

Go to your RCI softcover directory of resorts. The points values are color coded for the time of year, size of unit, and regional resort location.

In the RCI Directory of Resorts, RCI Weeks resorts are listed immediately following RCI Points resorts in each regional section. The regional sections and corresponding exchange grids are color-coded for easy reference.

To make an RCI Weeks reservation, log onto your account at

RCI.com or call an RCI Guide.

You should check with an RCI Guide before going ahead with a reservation just to confirm the exact amount of required points. If there is a point range printed on the chart, then RCI will also have to narrow down the actual point value.

Now - let's suppose that you want to vacation in France. We will use the world map method again.

<u>Click on Search for an Exchange Vacation.</u>

With your cursor, hover over Europe (the country turns a different   color when you hover over it) <u>and click on Europe</u>.
<u>Now, hover over France, and click on France.</u>
<u>Now click on select List View.</u>
<u>Now click on the green box to the right of</u>

Thalacap Ile Pere.

Use the upper right arrow on the monthly calendar(s) until you reach the desired month for your reservation. **Click on (Your choice).**

Your check-in and check-out dates will be displayed.

Click on the orange box that says select unit.

Click on the I acknowledge box.

Click on either cancel, confirm or hold.

Ongoing Search?

If you are searching for a vacation and don't find what you are looking for, click or tap "Start an Ongoing Search Request" in the box above your search results. Then, fill out the form with your desired criteria and continue to follow the prompts.

Again, what can you do if you can't make a future reservation at a destination of your choosing, and you are frustrated and ready to give up.

Ongoing search to the rescue. With an Ongoing Search, you key in your parameters (such as dates, destinations, even specific resorts) and the RCI software will continue searching for you 24/7. As new in inventory comes in, the ongoing search checks everything!

The really powerful thing about an ongoing search is that it searches all incoming inventory before it gets listed on RCI.com. You have a distinct reservation advantage by using the ongoing search option when making a future reservation.

An ongoing search scans everything until it finds exactly what you are looking for. When it finds exactly what you want, you are contacted and given the chance to book your dream vacation before the inventory is released to RCI.com.

CHAPTER 4

LAST CALL

FOUR WEEKS FOR ONE

What is the difference between **Last Call Vacations** and **Extra Vacations?**

Last Call vacations are last minute week-long getaways that are available to confirm within 45 days of check-in.

Last Call is a very inexpensive way to use your points to take many vacations when you have a limited number of points.

Last Call is a marketing plan where RCI affiliate Resorts realize that they have excess inventory that they won't be able rent through normal reservation channels. An analogy would be to a grocery story that has too many apples or oranges in stock. Instead of losing 100% of the value of this inventory, they mark it down, sometimes drastically before it becomes too late. Spoiled store inventory is worthless. With resorts, unsold inventory that moves past the check in date is worthless – it has absolutely -0- value.

Instead of taking a 100% hit on this excess (and what will become lost inventory and lost revenues) most affiliate resorts make it available to RCI members at a drastically reduced price (usually 9000 points or less). Last Call reservations can be made in the 2 – 45 day before check-in date.The goal in the hotel and resort industry is to aim at 0% vacancy at any given date. To achieve this they implement aggressive marketing plans to minimize vacancy levels.

If a resort has a 2-bedroom condo that normally requires 40,000 RCI points to reserve, in the Last Call program, this resort could be reserved for 9,000 points plus exchange fees.

Last Call opportunities can be paid for with cash even if you don't have any points. See Appendix "B" for reservation fees.

Secret: This is great way to get multiple vacation weeks for one week of ownership!

See appendix "A" for the Last Call reservation fees. Not all resorts participate in this program. The way to find out is to try to make a reservation in the 2 day to 45-day time period. If this resort participates in the Last Call program, the required number of points needed to complete the reservation will now be 9,000 points instead of 40,000 in some cases. Incredible value!

Take advantage of this benefit – it is easy to use and can provide a lot of extra value to your RCI Points membership! The author has used this benefit – and it works!

CHAPTER FIVE

EXTRA VACATIONS

What is the difference between last **Call Vacations**

and **Extra Vacations?**

Extra Vacations getaways are week-long vacations at RCI affiliated resorts, which are again resort promotions which can be purchased at incredible values.

You don't use any points for these reservations, transactions are cash or plastic. Extra Vacations getaways can be 3 star and 4 star resorts, and they are just like regular RCI exchange vacations.

You get the same spacious resort-style accommodations, benefits and amenities that you expect from a standard RCI vacation!

Pricing for Extra Vacations starts at $399 per week (USD). That comes out to $57 per night! **You can't stay at a cheap motel for this rate –Extra Vacations are an unbelievable value!**

Extra Vacation Benefits
> ➤ You don't use your points, you pay cash. No need to use your valuable points.
> ➤ New Extra Vacation opportunities become available every day!
> ➤ There is no limit to the number of Extra Vacations getaways you can take.
> ➤ Choose from a wide range of resorts and destinations around the world.
> ➤ You can add a Guest Certificate and give an Extra Vacations Getaway as a gift!

How to book an Extra Vacations getaway?
Simply log in to RCI.com to begin your search.

After logging in, check your My Offers box to see if you have any special offers. (If you don't have any offers available to you at the current time, the My Offers box will not appear. Check My Offers box daily, if not several times a day as Extra Vacations go fast.

Enhanced Search Tool

For other great deals, select "Extra Vacations Getaways" from the "Search for a Vacation" menu on www.rci.com. You can refine your search by applying up to 16 different filters.

Of course, you can always speak to an RCI Vacation Guide for help and guidance with booking your Extra Vacations getaway if you prefer.

Nightly Stays

Not looking to book a full 7 nights? You also have the flexibility to travel just a few nights or add an extra day to your trip. With budget-friendly prices, nightly stays are a great option for weekend trips, extra relaxation, or a quick escape.

CHAPTER SIX

POINTS PLATINUM

RCI PLATINUM MEMBERSHIP

To begin with, I will give you RCI's spin on their Platinum Points program. After their sales pitch, and review of the benefits offered in this program, I will spend some valuable page space on owner's comments from TUG (Timeshare Users Group). TUG is the largest independent Timeshare usefr group in the world, and postings on the TUG bulleting board are usually quite objective.

From RCI web site content:

City Attractions

Save 20% off things to do when you travel with a Go City Card multi-attraction pass. Passes include admission to top attractions, tours, museums, and more in 11 popular destinations for one low price. Pay nothing at the gate. More choices, more savings.

Complimentary Unit Upgrades & Changes

Here's how it works: when you book your confirmed Exchange vacation, you'll have the opportunity to receive Complimentary Unit Upgrades and Resort Changes. Just let us know you're interested in a unit upgrade or resort change. Within two weeks of check-in, if one of the resorts you've specified, or a bigger unit at your confirmed resort becomes available, we'll change your reservation and provide you with the details.

Savings Dollars

Earn Savings Dollars on select RCI transactions you already do (like paying exchange fees and renewing your RCI® subscribing membership).Then it's up to you how you redeem them – hotel stays, home electronics, fashion, wine (where legally available to ship), jewelry, sporting goods, dining certificates and more.*

Priority Access

Get exclusive access to exchange vacations at select hotels and resorts before they're made available to standard RCI® subscribing members for exchange.

RCI Platinum Points Extension

Get more time to enjoy your Points! As an RCI Platinum member, who is also an RCI Points® member, you are eligible to extend your unused Points for Two Use Years, as compared to standard RCI members who can extend their Points for only One Use Year, when they pay the same applicable fee. While extended Points expire at the end of a Third Use Year for standard RCI members, RCI Platinum members will enjoy a Fourth Use Year with no additional fee.

10% Discount on Extra VacationsSM getaways and Last CallSM Vacations

Enjoy an additional 10% off all your Extra VacationsSM getaways and Last CallSM Vacations — even those already on sale.*

Free Ongoing Search

Can't find the vacation you're looking for right now? We'll keep a lookout for you 24/7 and you won't be charged your exchange fee until we find a match!

Free On-Hold Vacations

Not quite ready to book? We'll hold your vacation for you without a fee while you iron out those last minute details.

Platinum Previews

RCI Platinum members have first dibs on Extra VacationsSM getaways sales! With RCI Platinum membership, see (and book) Extra Vacations getaways sales one day earlier than standard RCI

RCI Points Partner Program

Make your Points go farther! RCI Platinum members, who are RCI Points members, can use more of their annual Points allocation when booking travel – 50% of your annual Points allotment, rather than 33% for standard RCI members.

Platinum Cruise Exchange

RCI Platinum members still receive an extra $25USD off per cabin towards the purchase of select cruises (and can enjoy this benefit on an unlimited number of cabins, so bring along the whole family!)

Priority Answer

RCI Platinum members who call 1.866.545.7205 get quicker access to our knowledgeable guides. Enjoy fast answers from the RCI Platinum experts who are waiting to help you with your vacation planning!

Free Points Transfers

Know an RCI Points member that could use additional Points? Lucky them! Now RCI Platinum members no longer pay a Points transfer fee, so transfer away!

RCI Platinum® Guided Vacations

Looking to explore exotic locales? Or do you want to visit renowned golf, ski, and spa destinations in the U.S.? Either way, we've got a vacation tour for you! Plus, RCI Platinum members receive an extra $25USD per couple towards the purchase of select tours, as compared to standard RCI members.

Timeshare User's Group

Comments from Users Who Have Been Platinum Members

We generally book several extra vacations a year. I like getting 10% off those. I like the one day advance notice of sales as well...I've often nabbed something on that day that wasn't there when the sale opened up to everyone else. I've not investigated the savings dollars...that's not really why I signed up, so didn't bother looking into them.

In general there [it] looks like a [the] max you can spend on a hotel depending on price. For example I have over $400 in savings dollars. I looked at a local hotel and even though I could use a rate that would be just under $100 booking direct with the hotel as a rewards member of that chain, even if I use the same rate code on RCI and starwood.com and using the max $31 savings dollars I would be saving about $8 over the direct booked rate. My guess is I would lose ability to earn points over that $8 for the stay.

I wouldn't expect to save more than $50 per night using the saving dollars and the higher end only when staying at select high end hotels that probably have other ways to get equal savings.

Details from users is a bit different than RCI's take on the deal. I was told you could use the Savings Dollars to pay for the entire hotel room with only a $20 -$25 booking fee, even when I asked if there was a limit on how much Saving $$ can be applied I was told I could pay pay for the whole thing...... 100% off of Extra vacation stays is good if you do many...Again Thank you, it is good to ask the real users for the real deal....

The price probably depends on the hotel, the area, and the demand. My experience the couple times I looked was that the RCI price was nearly the same as the expedia price. Then I could use a set amount of savings dollars to reduce the price anywhere from 10-30% below the expedia price. The exact number of dollars that could be used and percentage savings varied by hotel.

CHAPTER 7

LUXURY
THE REGISTRY COLLECTION

The Registry Collection

What is "The Registry Collection?

Here is a very brief and to the point explanation. The Registry Collection (Hereafter referred to as THC) is a separate travel company that has access to a somewhat confidential association/selection of high end and extremely luxurious resorts around the world. These prestigious and elegant resorts are for those RCI Points members who have a lot of RCI Points.

How do you go about making a reservation at one of these exclusive destinations?

To begin with you must become a member of THC. Membership is $250 for one year.

Secondly, you must deposit and convert the RCI Points value of one or more your RCI Points based ownerships to TRC credits in order to make a reservation. To accomplish this, you must call a TRC reservation person in order to find out how many credits your points are worth.

Depending on what TRC you want to make a reservation at, you should probably have an extra 100 thousand to 200 thousand points that you are about to lose, or are willing to trade for pure luxury.

Thirdly, to make a reservation at a TRC destination, it will cost you an additional exchange fee with TRC. That is on top of the normal exchange fee charged by RCI.

To put things into the proper perspective, the dollar value of a reservation at a TRC resort will be much higher than a normal RCI reservation. The price of pure luxury.

If you have the money and the points, and want to vacation at one of the most incredible resorts in the world, just do it.

The reservation agents and concierges at THC will be a critical piece of the puzzle, as they must compute the points to credits conversion, and handle the conversion to credits if you decide to go ahead and make a reservation.

The concierge is a second extremely important piece of the puzzle. They are tasked with putting together an unforgettable and once in a lifetime vacation adventure.

Here are more benefits and advantages of this incredible program.

When you become a member and make your first reservation, you will have access to a personalized concierge service. TRC describes this personalized concierge service as one of the most important and valuable benefits of their program.

Your concierge has one major goal in life – that is to do everything possible and imaginable to make you vacation a memorable one.

They will set up custom tours, yacht rentals, car rentals, and reservations at exclusive and hard to get into restaurants.

If there are special things that you want to do on your vacation (Iif legal), they will make it happen. They will try to make sure that you will have the vacation of a lifetime!

The RCI/and The Registry Collection "Spin"

"The Registry Collection – Your Key to the Ultimate in Luxury Vacations"

Now you can utilize your RCI Points and RCI Points membership to gain access to some of the most beautiful and luxurious resorts in the world.

Your RCI Points and Points Membership make it possible to now have "Luxury Ownership". Your luxury ownership is an investment in the best things in life. The Registry Collection® program offers you a world of exclusivity, privilege, and superlative quality, expanding your leisure choices with a portfolio of many of the finest vacation properties and services around the world.

The Registry Collection program provides valuable lifestyle resources—from the Collection Partners, featuring international golf travel, yacht charters, custom travel packages, and other premium travel services, to The Registry Collection program's travel Concierge Services, providing 24-7 assistance with your travel arrangements.

Welcome to The Registry Collection program where, as a valued member, you can look forward to outstanding value, extraordinary selection, and the ultimate vacation experiences.

The Registry Collection Program rules may vary by region and membership type. For complete program rules and benefits please contact your local Reservation Consultant.

Questions and answers about the "The Registry Collection"

Q: If I book a Reservation through The Registry Collection® program and something happens where I have to cancel or change the dates/location, what are my options?

A: If you have a confirmed a Reservation that has to be changed or cancelled, you will forfeit your transaction fee and possibly a portion of your Credits. However, as a member of The Registry Collection program you can protect your Credits by purchasing Credit Protection. Credit Protection must be purchased within 30 days of booking, and at least 30 days prior to the start date of the Reservation.

Q: Why does your Web site indicate that a property has availability, but when I call I'm sometimes told it is no longer available?

A: Our availability grid is updated daily Monday through Friday, consequently, the listed availability does not display in "real time." Because it can change by the minute, please call a Reservation Consultant to obtain the most current status and exact check-in dates available.

Q: How do I view available locations on The Registry Collection program website? Is it real time availability?

A: We offer a great tool on our website that allows you to preview a sample of available luxury travel experiences. Log on to our website homepage (www.theregistrycollection.com). In the left navigation bar is you will find the button "Availability". Click on it and it will take you to a page where you can view a date of availability by property. Although this is not updated in real-time, it is a snap shot of availability at the start of each business day. Many members have found this to be a helpful vacation planning tool.

Q: How long are my Credits available for use?

A: You may deposit your Interval as early as one year prior to the start-date of the Interval. Once your deposit information has been verified by your resort, the Credits are placed in your account and are immediately available for an exchange. A deposited interval with a start-date that begins within the current year means the Credits are eligible until December 31st of the following year. A deposited interval with a start-date that begins within a future year means the Credits are eligible until December 31st of the subsequent year.

Q: How do I increase the likelihood of exchanging through The Registry Collection program?

A: Depositing your Interval and submitting your vacation request as early as possible, having flexibility in terms of travel dates and alternative locations, and being open to a variety of travel experiences help to increase the likelihood that you will find an exchange. Please discuss the Ongoing Search option with your Reservation Consultant to increase your exchange abilities further. Don't hesitate to call, we are here to provide you with vacation planning advice.

Q: Why are my deposits final transactions?

A: As soon as your deposit is verified by your home property, it is immediately available for exchange and is able to be immediately reserved by another member to satisfy their vacation request. Members' deposit of their Intervals is how we send members of The Registry Collection program on their dream vacations! Therefore, it's important that you (as well as the owners of the properties that you may be interested in) deposit your Interval as soon as you know you'd like to vacation somewhere else.

Q: Does The Registry Collection program have any travel-related options for me if I choose not to deposit my Interval?

A: Absolutely! As a member of The Registry Collection program you have access to several non-exchange, luxury travel-related service providers known as Collection Partners. These companies provide special pricing, added service benefits and unique opportunities that are consistent with a vacation experience in The Registry Collection program. Please call one of our Reservation Consultants to take advantage of the relationships that have been established to be connected with one of our Collection Partners today!

Adventures by Disney
(http://www.adventuresbydisney.com)

European Villas and Manors
(www.cottageselection.co.uk/rgc)

Fairmont Hotels & Resorts
(http://www.fairmont.com/promotions/registrycollectio

n)

James Villa Holidays
(https://www.jamesvillas.co.uk/)

Priority Pass
(www.prioritypass.com/registrycollection)

PerryGolf (www.perrygolf.com)

Yachtstore
(www.theregistrycollection.yachtstore.com)

Q: What are the benefits of an Ongoing Search?

A: The Registry Collection program exchange
process works on a first-come, first-serve basis.
Members deposit their intervals at varying times;
therefore, being on a Ongoing Search allows us to offer
a member available inventory that they are interested in
as it comes into our system. Finally, members on the
Ongoing Search list do not have to repeatedly call The
Registry Collection program to check availability.
Remember, you may request to be placed on The
Registry Collection program's Ongoing Search 365
days prior to your desired travel date(s).

Q: How far in advance can I book reservations or begin an Ongoing Search?

A: Members can reserve vacations, or begin an Ongoing Search if the desired location is not immediately available, up to one year in advance of the check-in date. We encourage our members to plan one year in advance to have the most success in obtaining their desired vacation.

Q: How will I know when a vacation opportunity becomes available from a Ongoing Search?

A: All Ongoing Searches are managed through our computerized database which continuously searches to find you the vacation opportunity that meets the criteria indicated to the Reservation Consultant. This is monitored on a daily basis and if your desired vacation becomes available, a Reservation Consultant will either telephone or email you—whichever you prefer—with the details.

Q:What if there isn't availability at one of The Registry Collection properties in the area where I want to vacation?

A: The Registry Collection® program is pleased to offer our members access to more than 500 resorts representing nearly 40 locations that are associated with RCI's vacation exchange network. Achieving RCI's highest quality award, the Gold Crown, along with consistent above average RCI member comment card scores, the associate resorts offer a vacation exchange alternative located in sought after locations. While the experience may be different than that of a Collection property, these resort vacation alternatives meet the standards of The Registry Collection program - providing you with even more vacation opportunities in destinations around the world.

CHAPTER 8

POINTS PARTNERS

The RCI Points Partner Program allows certain RCI Points subscribing members to exchange a portion of their Points for discounts on the value of a wide range of travel products including flights, hotel stays, car rentals and more.

HOW MANY POINTS CAN I USE IN THE RCI POINTS PARTNER PROGRAM?

As a general rule, in a calendar year, members may use an amount equal to 33% of their annual Points allotment (up to a maximum of 250,000 Points) or 25,000 Points, whichever is greater. RCI Platinum® members may use a higher proportion of their Points in the program - an amount equal to 50% of their annual Points allotment (up to a maximum of 250,000 Points) or 40,000 Points, whichever is greater. Some additional terms and conditions may apply for members who own at certain resorts - please click here for details.

HOW MANY RCI POINTS PARTNER

TRANSACTIONS CAN I MAKE IN A YEAR?

Provided that you have sufficient Points remaining which are eligible to use in the RCI Points Partner program, there is no limit to the number of Transactions that you can make.

DO I HAVE TO BE AN RCI POINTS SUBSCRIBING MEMBER TO USE THE RCI POINTS PARTNER PROGRAM?

Yes. To make a Points Partner Transaction, you must be a current RCI Points subscribing member who is eligible to participate in the Points Partner program and be up to date with any fees related to your membership.

CAN I BORROW POINTS FROM MY NEXT USE YEAR TO MAKE RCI POINTS PARTNER TRANSACTIONS?

Yes, but this does not increase the overall number of Points you can use in the RCI Points Partner program in any given calendar year. As a general rule, the number of Points you can use in the RCI Points Partner program is based on your annual Points allocation. Some additional terms and conditions may apply for members who own at certain resorts - please click here for details.

CAN I RENT (AS THIS TERMS IS REFERRED TO IN THE TERMS AND CONDITIONS OF RCI POINTS SUBSCRIBING MEMBERSHIP) POINTS TO COMPLETE RCI POINTS PARTNER TRANSACTIONS?

No.

WHAT DISCOUNTS DO I RECEIVE FOR MY POINTS?

Discounts will vary by product type, price and timing of the RCI Points Partner opportunities, and will require a minimum number of Points for each RCI Points Partner Transaction. Members will have online access at www.rci.com to the most current RCI Points Partner Discounts. In addition, RCI guides will be available, at 1-877-968-7476 or other numbers published by RCI from time to time, to assist Members. All Discounts remain subject to change without notice at the sole discretion of RCI. Simply select your desired product, and as you check out you will have the option to select how many Points you wish to use (subject to the required minimum), and will be shown the discount.

AM I LIMITED TO USING SPECIFIC THRESHOLDS OF POINTS AMOUNTS?

Each Points Partner transaction has a minimum number of Points that must be applied towards the purchase. If you use more than the minimum amount, you will be able to use any number of Points in increments of one Point to the maximum allowed per year and for that particular Points Partner transaction.

WHAT TRANSACTION FEES APPLY?

The transaction fees for RCI Points Partner reservations are as follows:

Online (USD)
Product
Airline Tickets $25 per ticket
Car Rental $25 per car
Entertainment Tickets $25 per ticket
Hotels (Preferred and Standard) $25 per room

WHY IS THE TRANSACTION FEE LOWER WHEN I BOOK ONLINE?

The costs to RCI associated with online bookings are lower.

DOES MY RCI POINTS PARTNER TRANSACTION COVER EVERYTHING WHICH MAY BE PAYABLE?

In some cases, additional charges from a third party provider may apply. This may include incidental charges, such as parking and internet service at hotels, or insurance, gas, tax and GPS hire when booking a rental car.

I HAVE A COUPON CODE FOR ONE OF THE THIRD PARTY PROVIDERS WHICH PARTICIPATES IN THE RCI POINTS PARTNER PROGRAM - CAN I USE IT?

No. Additional offers such as coupon codes from third party providers cannot be used in conjunction with offers in the RCI Points Partner program.

CAN I MAKE SPECIAL REQUESTS WITH HOTELS OR AIRLINES WITH REGARD TO MY RCI POINTS PARTNER BOOKING?

If you have any special requirements for your booking (such as late check-in or handicapped access) you should always contact the third party vendor directly.

CAN I APPLY MY FREQUENT FLYER ACCOUNT TO MY AIR RESERVATION TO EARN AIR MILES?

Yes, simply add the relevant account information when you are prompted to do so during the online booking process. This information will be passed on to the airline, but it is recommended that you check with the airline when you check-in that your information has been added to your booking correctly. Frequent flyer miles cannot be used to pay for any portion of your RCI Points Partner Transaction.

CAN I APPLY MY HOTEL REWARD PROGRAM NUMBER TO MY HOTEL RESERVATION?

Not at this time. If you wish to apply your hotel reward number to a reservation, you should do so directly with the hotel, either by calling or at check-in. This is always dependent on the hotel's own policies.

CAN I CANCEL OR CHANGE MY RESERVATION?

No. All RCI Points Partner Transactions are completely non-refundable, non-changeable, and non-transferable and are subject to terms of conditions of the RCI Points Partner program, as well as the terms and conditions of the third party provider. Any cash paid to supplement Points or to pay Transaction fees will not be refunded. Points are non-refundable.

I FOUND THE SAME THING CHEAPER ELSEWHERE, DO YOU PRICE-MATCH?

If you find a lower rate on another U.S. based website within 24 hours of booking, for the same product you purchased, you can receive the difference, per the terms of the Best Rate Guarantee.

WHEN I MAKE A POINTS PARTNER TRANSACTION ONLINE, IS IT INSTANTLY CONFIRMED?

In some cases such Transactions are placed in a pending status while being confirmed by the airline. You will always receive an email confirmation when your transaction is confirmed. Also note that while your Transaction has been confirmed, your name may not be added to a hotel reservation system until closer to your arrival date.

DOES RCI PROVIDE ALL THE PRODUCTS AND SERVICES AVAILABLE THROUGH THE RCI POINTS PARTNER PROGRAM?

No. Products and services available through the RCI Points Partner program are all provided by third parties via International OVC Our Vacation Center . Information about RCI Points Partner products and services published by RCI is based on information obtained from the applicable RCI Points Partner third party vendor. In addition to the terms of conditions of the RCI Points Partner program, your RCI Points Partner Transactions are also subject to the terms and conditions of the applicable RCI Points Partner.

CAN A GUEST USE A RESERVATION I MAKE USING THE RCI POINTS PARTNER PROGRAM?

Yes, you can purchase a Guest Certificate for any of the travel services offered through the RCI Points Partner program if you are not a part of the traveling party.

I MADE A RESERVATION THROUGH THE RCI POINTS PARTNER PROGRAM, AND HAVE A CHARGE ON MY CREDIT CARD FROM "OUR VACATION STORE", WHAT IS THIS CHARGE?

The services provided through the RCI Points Partner program are provided via a third party. This charge is for the cash component required as a part of the RCI Points Partner Transaction (including the RCI Transaction fee).

CAN I USE MY TRAVEL REWARDS TOWARD THE CASH PORTION OF AN RCI POINTS PARTNER TRANSACTION?

Yes. Travel Rewards may be used toward payment of a Points Partner transaction (excluding the RCI Transaction fee), under the following rules (prices are in USD):

A minimum of $15 Travel Rewards must be used towards any Hotel booking
A minimum of $15 Travel Rewards must be used towards any Car Rental
A minimum of $25 Travel Rewards must be used towards any Airline Ticket
A minimum of $15 Travel Rewards must be used towards any Theme Park Ticket purchase

a max you can spend on a hotel depending on price. For example I have over $400 in savings dollars. I looked at a local hotel and even though I could use a rate that would be just under $100 booking direct with the hotel as a rewards member of that chain, even if I use the same rate code on RCI and starwood.com and using the max $31 savings dollars I would be saving about $8 over the direct booked rate. My guess is I would lose ability to earn points over that $8 for the stay.

"I wouldn't expect to save more than $0-$50 per night using the saving dollars and the higher end only when staying at select high end hotels that probably have other ways to get equal savings"

"Thank you for the info, as I guessed the real details from users is a bit different than RCI's take on the deal. I was told you could use the Savings Dollars to pay for the entire hotel room with only a $20 -$25 booking fee, even when I asked if there was a limit on how much Saving $$ can be applied I was told no you can pay for the whole thing" Again Thank you, it is good to ask the real users for the real deal...."

"The price probably depends on the hotel, the area, and the demand. My experience the couple times I looked was that the RCI price was nearly the same as the expedia price. Then I could use a set amount of savings dollars to reduce the price anywhere from 10-30% below the expedia price. The exact number of dollars that could be used and percentage savings varied by hotel."

"I thought restaurant.com was gone too or at least I had to use saving dollars to purchase them. They still seem to be available one in my weeks account and one in my points account available each month."

CHAPTER 9 – CRUISE VACATIONS

How to Book an RCI Cruise – using RCI Points

Log in to your RCI member account--you'll need to be logged in to book a cruise using RCI Points. Point your web browser to RCI.com, enter your username and password, and click "Points Sign In."

Click "Travel Resources," then scroll down to the bottom of the page and click "RCI Cruise." Scroll through the options for "Destination," "Duration," "Cruise Line" and "Sailing Date," then click "Search Cruises" to see available options that meet your specifications. Click "See Details" to learn more about cruises that interest you.

Click the price of the cruise, then "Select Cabin," then enter passenger details including name, address, RCI Point ID and citizenship. Customize your cruise -- add additional ports of call, for instance, or pre-book entertainment and dining options -- then proceed on to the "Payment" screen by clicking "Continue." Click "Pay Using Points," then complete your transaction.

Call 866-728-0729 if you experience difficulties using the website, or if you simply prefer booking a cruise with the help of an RCI customer service person.

The following information is the RCI "spin" on using RCI Points for cruises.

Four Great Reasons to Book with RCI Cruise

1. Special Offers & Discounts

RCI Cruise guides have exclusive access to deals and discounts that aren't available to consumers booking directly. They often can offer complimentary bottles of wine, vouchers for specialty dining, prepaid gratuities, and onboard credits. These offers are in addition to already low member rates. When you combine the two, you know you're getting the absolute best value. We're so confident this will be the case, we offer the RCI Cruise Best Rate Guarantee1.

2. Knowledgeable Guides

RCI Cruise guides can offer a wealth of information with plenty of real world travel experience. Cruise guides can provide incredible advice for making the most of a cruise, including insight into the best onboard dining venues or cruise ship activities for children, as well as expertise on travel insurance, dining times and cabin location. For first-time cruisers, speaking with a cruise guide is a must. Even the experienced cruiser can benefit from a cruise guide's advice.

3. Stress Less, Relax More

There are many details that go into planning a cruise vacation. Why worry about them when RCI subscribing members automatically have access to experienced cruise guides? Let a guide dot the i's and cross the t's on your vacation. From completing your booking exactly as you want it, to arranging your pre and post cruise hotel, to giving you first-hand tips and advice, your experience will be hassle-free, allowing you to truly relax and unwind at sea.

4. One-Stop Vacation Planning

Today there are more cruise vacation choices and experiences than ever before, making it possible for travel agents to tailor trips to each member's travel preferences. Take the example of a couple wanting to plan their dream cruise through the rivers of France. A cruise guide can help book the perfect Parisian cruise and even provide tips for finding the best crepes and macarons during onshore excursions

CHAPTER 10

MANAGING YOUR POINTS

Managing Your Points – a challenging scenario.

Here is an interesting scenario. You have taken two weeks of vacation by using "Last Call in your current use year, and you still have 30,000 points remaining. If you don't use these points, they will eventually go away. The overly used Timeshare axioms says "Use them or lose them". There is much truth to this logic. If your points go away or are unused, it is just like throwing money away. You don't have to lose your points or use them inefficiently.

The information in this chapter will show you unique, or unknown, or non-advertised ways of maximizing your investment in RCI Points. Here are some Tips, Tricks and Secret ways to better utilize your points.

There are two major things to consider before perusing the following.

- First of all, you should never, never, never, lose your points by letting them expire. Don't let that happen! Below you will find bullets next to many (but not all) of the ways you can use your points more efficiently and even extend your usage years.

- Secondly, never, never, never cancel or chose not to make vacation or travel arrangements because you think that you don't have enough points. That just doesn't hold water and is an irrational and erroneous way to think Please read the options below! You will find many new ways to find vacation options that you thought didn't exist

What can I do if my Points are close to Expiring?

- With your unused points, you can take a short getaway trip for 2,3,4,5, or 6 days. You don't have to use your points for a full week.

- You can use your extra points to send a friend

or family member on vacation.

- You can extend your points – up to three years in some cases.

- Read on to find methods of finding additional points in order to make your vacation reservations. For example, if your current Point balance is 24,000 Points, but your desired exchange vacation is valued at 30,000 Points, you can Borrow the extra 6,000 Points from your next Use Year.

- In the Extend Points box you'll see your number of Points eligible to be Extended and directions on how to proceed.

- You can use your spare points buy a gift certificate and use it as a birthday or wedding present.

- The points you don't use are automatically saved into a second "Use Year". However, if you haven't used any points in the current year, RCI will still rollover your points, but there will be a $26 fee applied.

- RCI Platinum members are allowed an additional use year before their points expire.

- You can also extend your points into a 3rd year,. A fee will be applied based on the number of points you want to roll-over.

- How to extend points. Sign in to your account at RCI.com and access Account Details under Home in the main navigation. In the Extend Points box you'll see your number of Points eligible to be "Extended" and directions on how to proceed.

- When booking an exchange vacation with a check-in date in your next Use Year, and you have Points eligible to be extended for use on that transaction, you'll see the option to do so during the exchange vacation checkout process.

- If you don't want to lose your points, look in the Extend Points box. You will see the number of Points eligible to be Extended and the directions on how to proceed.

- You can always transfer your extra or unused points to another RCI Points subscriber. A transfer fee will apply.

- You can rent points if you don't have enough points to complete a reservation for your dream vacation. The rental points must be used in your current "Use Year". *The rental rate and the Renting Points feature may change from time to time without notice. Your ability to rent Points will depend on the availability of vacations in the RCI Points program. Rented Points may only be used in the current Use Year.

- To initiate a "Renting Points" transaction, you need to call your RCI vacation counselor. You can rent points every "Use Year". You can rent the equivalent up to 50% of your regular allotment of points, once per use year.

- After you have chosen your vacation destination, and have come up short on the needed, the following will happen. You will be prompted as to whether you want to rent or borrow points to complete the transaction. Or you can chose to do neither, which might not be a wise decision.

- To proceed, you would need to call your RCI Vacation guide and let them know if you want to rent or borrow points.

- Rented points can only be used in your current "Use Year".

- Follow this link to find a listing of all member fees

- https://www.rci.com/pre-rci-en_US/help/forms-and-fees/pow-member-fees-us.page.

- Points for deposit. Even if your week is already deposited in the RCI Weeks exchange program, if it is eligible for Points for Deposit, you can still take advantage of this program. You can convert up to 4 eligible weeks per resort per calendar year to Points through the Points for Deposit program.

- Points® for Deposit allows RCI Points® subscribing members, who also own an eligible week at an RCI Weeks affiliated resort, to deposit that week with RCI and receive Points for that deposit. They can then use those Points in the RCI Points exchange program.

- Points for eligible -The Points you receive for your week will be allocated to the Use Year in which the start date of the week you are depositing falls, and it can take up to 15 days for the Points to be deposited into your account.

NOTE: Your "Use Year" is a recurring 12 month period that starts on the first of the month following the setup or initiation of your RCI account.

APPENDIX A – FEES

RCI® Points Fees United States July 1, 2018

The following information details the various fees

that are associated with your membership benefits.

Usually, on an annual basis, you will also pay a maintenance fee, which is used towards the operation and upkeep of the resort at which you own. This is not a fee which is collected by RCI - you pay this fee to your resort directly.

Please note: New fees associated with your membership will go into effect on December 1, 2018. View Changes.

Annual RCI Points® Subscription Fees USD

	Total Cost (USD)	Price Per Year (USD)
1 YR	$124	
2 YRS	$229	
3 YRS	$321	
4 YRS	$409	
5 YRS	$499	

Annual RCI Points Platinum Fees

	Total Cost (USD)	Price Per Year (USD)
RCI Points Platinum® 1 Yr	$89	
RCI Points Platinum® 2 Yrs	$155	$77.50
RCI Points Platinum® 3 Yrs	$221	$73.67
RCI Points Platinum® 4 Yrs	$279	$69.75
RCI Points Platinum® 5 Yrs	$322	

$64.40

Gold Membership Fees	Total Cost (USD)	Price Per Year (USD)
1 YR	$49	
2 YRS	$86	$43
3 YRS	$123	$41
4 YRS	$156	$39
5 YRS	$180	$36

Exchange Vacations	USD (Call Center/RCI.com)
Home Week Reservation (7 nights)	No Charge
Home Resort Reservation (7 nights)	$50
RCI Points Reservation 14 nights +	$288
RCI Points Reservation: 7-13 nights	$209
RCI Points Reservation 6 nights	$199
RCI Points Reservation:5 nights	$179
RCI Points Reservation 4 nights	$139
RCI Points Reservation:3 nights	$109
RCI Points Reservation 2 nights	$79
RCI Points Reservation: 1 night	$59
RCI Weeks Reservation (7 nights)	$239

RCI Points Partner Program

	USD (On-line - RCI.com)	SD (call center)
Air (per ticket)	$25	$52
Car (per car)	$25	$52
Entertainment (per ticket/pass)	$25	$39
Hotels (per room)	$25	$52

Managing Your Points	USD
Points Saving Fee	$26
Points Extension - Less than or Equal to 30,000 Points	$85
Points Extension - 30,001 Points or more	$125

Points Rental Fee (Per Point)	$0.03
Points for Deposit Fee	$49

RCI Points Protection

Purchased 30 days or less from the date of vacation confirmation AND 15 days or more before check-in date   USD

1-2 nights	$39
3-4 nights	$49
5+ nights	$59

Purchased 31 days or more from the date of vacation confirmation OR 14 days or less from check-in date

USD

1-2 nights	$79
3-4 nights	$89
5+ nights	$99

Miscellaneous Fees (USD)
Guest Certificates $84
Membership Transfer Application $98
Duplicate Points Directory (S&H) $6.95

RCI fees are subject to change at RCI's sole discretion. For complete details of RCI subscribing membership, including RCI's cancellation policy, please consult the Terms and Conditions of RCI Points® Subscribing Membership.

APPENDIX B

TIMESHARE TERMINOLOGY

Banking or Deposit – Depositing a week of Timeshare into an exchange system or inventory pool.

Biennial – Use of a Timeshare week every other year. Owners are often referred to as either "odd" or "even" year owners.

Developer – The company owning the resort. Responsible for constructing the accommodations on-site and selling the product.

Exchange Company – The system that allows Timeshare owners to trade the accommodations they own for comparable accommodations or travel-related services. Most resort companies are affiliated with an exchange company. Many resort companies offer an internal exchange mechanism that allows owners to exchange to resorts within their company's portfolio of resorts.

Fixed week – A type of Timeshare ownership in which usage rights attach to a specific week of the year each year in perpetuity.

Floating week – A type of Timeshare ownership where the use rights are subject to the owner reserving his or her week within a season purchased (winter, summer, etc.) or sometimes throughout the year. A year-round "float" is most often found in resorts with similar seasons, like Hawaii or the Caribbean.

Fractional Ownership – Leisure real estate sold in intervals of more than one week and less than whole ownership. Fractionals are usually associated with the luxury segment of vacation ownership, offering greater services and amenities.

Home Owners Association (HOA) – The group of owners that administer the rules and regulations of a resort. Creation of an HOA is often required by state laws.

Home resort – The resort location where a new purchaser owns his or her week or designated as the home resort in a club or points-based program. Ownership is usually tied to this home resort and generally involves priority reservation rights in that location.

Interval or weekly interval – Vacation ownership as measured by a set number of days and nights of annual use, usually one week.

Lock-off – A type of Timeshare unit consisting of multiple living and sleeping quarters designed to function as two discrete units for purposes of occupancy and exchange. The unit can be combined to form one large unit or can be split or "locked-off" into two or more separate unites, allowing the owner to split the vacation into multiple stays or bank all or a portion for exchange purposes.

Maintenance fee – A fee that Timeshare owners are required to pay, usually on an annual basis, to cover the costs of running the resort, including daily management, upkeep, and improvements.

Points – A "currency" that represents Timeshare ownership and is used to establish value for seasons, unit sizes, and resort locations. Points are used by some developers for both internal and external exchange.

Points conversion program – An offering whereby owners of a Timeshare interval(s) pay(s) a fee to convert their interval for the equivalent in points.

Rescission – Sometimes called a "cancellation" or "cooling off" period. A period of time during which a consumer has the right to cancel a purchase contract and obtain a full refund of his/her deposit with no penalty. Dictated by state statute and company policy, rescission periods vary from state to state, but range on average from 5 to 7 days. This is another example of the strong consumer protections built into the Timeshare sales.

Resale – A vacation ownership interest that is sold on the secondary market by the original purchaser to a third party.

Right to use – A Timeshare owner's right to occupy a unit at a resort for a specified number of years and having no real estate interest conveyed.

Timesharing – A term used to describe a method of use and/or shared ownership of vacation real estate where purchasers acquire a period of time (often one week) in a condominium, apartment or other type of vacation accommodation. Timeshare is also known as "vacation ownership."

Trading power – A term used for the value assigned for exchange purposes to a member's deposited vacation time.

Trial membership – A product offered after the initial sales tour consisting of travel-related products and services packaged with an opportunity to experience the resort developer's primary vacation ownership product within a defined period. Sometimes called a "sampler" program.

Vacation Club – A term used to describe various types of timesharing and usually involving use or access to more than one resort location and other vacation and travel services. However, the term is used for many different purposes, including "clubs" which may have nothing to do with timesharing.

Vacation ownership – A term often used to describe resort timesharing.

APPENDIX C

IMPORTANT PRESS RELEASES

FOR IMMEDIATE RELEASE

RCI Expands its Global Vacation Offerings with More Than 135 New Resorts in 2017

The largest vacation exchange network added approximately 80 international properties in 2017 to its global network of over 4,300 affiliated resorts

PARSIPPANY, N.J. (February 21, 2018) – RCI, the global leader in vacation exchange and part of the Wyndham Worldwide family of brands (NYSE:

WYN), welcomed more than 135 newly affiliated resorts to its exchange network in 2017. These additions span across every populated continent and feature vacation experiences with great options for nearly every kind of journey, from surf and sun to glittering modern cities.

"Over the past year, we've added some exceptional properties to the RCI® exchange network," said Gordon Gurnik, president, RCI. "Through strategic partnerships with both new and existing affiliates, our 3.8 million subscribing members have thousands of options to choose from in sought-after destinations around the world when planning their next vacation."

In Latin America, RCI added more than 55 resorts, many of which are in notable beach destinations. The Ventus at Marina El Cid Spa & Beach Resort is located in the quaint fishing village of Puerto Morelos, Mexico, along the gorgeous Mayan Rivera. In addition to the beautiful views of the Caribbean Sea, guests can also enjoy the luxurious resort amenities and local cultural experiences from the ancient Mayans that used to inhabit the area.

RCI also enjoyed outstanding growth in the Asia-Pacific region with more than 20 new resorts.
Emerald Terrace Condominium Resort in Phuket, Thailand, is one of the most recent additions. Located on a lush hillside, the resort island is full of tranquil

delights and scenic adventures from elephant treks through the untouched jungle to scuba diving the colorful local playgrounds of marine life.

The company's North American footprint expanded by nearly 50 resorts in 2017 as well. One of these additions includes the Prestige Collection Harbourside at Marker 33 in Indian Rocks Beach, Florida, which offers many family-friendly activities. The resort shares the grounds with Splash Harbour Water Park, and features a 42 foot tall tube slide, single rider body slide, 600 foot relaxing lazy river, extra-large sundeck and zero-entry pool with mushroom waterfalls and ground sprays. The water park also features a splash zone, game room and 18 holes of tropical themed miniature golf.

FOR IMMEDIATE RELEASE

RCI Expands its Global Vacation Offerings with More Than 135 New Resorts in 2017

The largest vacation exchange network added approximately 80 international properties in 2017 to its global network of over 4,300 affiliated resorts

PARSIPPANY, N.J. (February 21, 2018) – RCI, the global leader in vacation exchange and part of the Wyndham Worldwide family of brands (NYSE: WYN), welcomed more than 135 newly affiliated resorts to its exchange network in 2017. These additions span across every populated continent and feature vacation experiences with great options for nearly every kind of journey, from surf and sun to glittering modern cities.

"Over the past year, we've added some exceptional properties to the RCI® exchange network," said Gordon Gurnik, president, RCI. "Through strategic partnerships with both new and existing affiliates, our 3.8 million subscribing members have thousands of options to choose from in sought-after destinations around the world when planning their next vacation."

In Latin America, RCI added more than 55 resorts, many of which are in notable beach destinations. The Ventus at Marina El Cid Spa & Beach Resort is located in the quaint fishing village of Puerto Morelos, Mexico, along the gorgeous Mayan Rivera. In addition to the beautiful views of the Caribbean Sea, guests can also enjoy the luxurious resort amenities and local cultural experiences from the ancient Mayans that used to inhabit the area.

RCI also enjoyed outstanding growth in the Asia-

Pacific region with more than 20 new resorts.

Emerald Terrace Condominium Resort in Phuket, Thailand, is one of the most recent additions. Located on a lush hillside, the resort island is full of tranquil delights and scenic adventures from elephant treks through the untouched jungle to scuba diving the colorful local playgrounds of marine life.

The company's North American footprint expanded by nearly 50 resorts in 2017 as well. One of these additions includes the Prestige Collection Harbourside at Marker 33 in Indian Rocks Beach, Florida, which offers many family-friendly activities. The resort shares the grounds with Splash Harbour Water Park, and features a 42 foot tall tube slide, single rider body slide, 600 foot relaxing lazy river, extra-large sundeck and zero-entry pool with mushroom waterfalls and ground sprays. The water park also features a splash zone, game room and 18 holes of tropical themed miniature golf.

RCI Adds Two New Resorts to Affiliate Network in China

Singapore (September 27, 2017) - RCI, the worldwide leader in vacation exchange (NYSE: WYN), recently welcomed two new affiliate resorts in China to its exchange network - Blue Bay International Resort and Fujian Wuyi Hot Spring Resort. With these additions, RCI's portfolio in China now boasts over 60 properties. This agreement allows 3.8 million RCI members to access vacation exchanges in China.

"We believe that timeshare is currently the new preferred way of consumer leisure travel and are confident that our partnership with RCI will boost Hooray Island's presence in the international market. We know that RCI is the right partner for our brand given its 40 years in the business," said Mr. Luo, CEO of Hooray Island Resorts World.

"Vacation ownership continues to lead in the hospitality and leisure industry with steady growth, and China continues to be one of our core markets," said Jonathan Mills, managing director of RCI Asia Pacific.

"I am delighted to announce these new affiliations, underscoring RCI's focus on developing this market."

The new affiliated properties include:

1. Blue Bay International Resort

Located in the Gulei Economic Development Zone in the south coast of Zhangzhou, Fujian, Blue Bay International Resort features scenic beaches, lush forests and tranquil lakes. In addition to its beautiful natural surroundings, the resort also boasts an 18-hole championship golf course with premium golf club amenities, five-star hotel accommodation and MICE facilities, an RV campsite, a world-class water theme park and a yacht club. With the completion of the Coastal Chase Road targeted to end by 2018, Blue Bay International Resort will be a 50-min drive away from Xiamen.

2. Fujian Wuyi Hot Spring Resort

Fujian Wuyi Hot Spring Resort is a well-designed boutique resort hotel located in Wuyishan, the southeastern part of China, a popular destination for domestic travelers. Comprising 25 units scheduled to open end 2017, each unit is equipped with en-suite hot spring tubs, in-room sauna and spa facilities. The resort boasts two on-site restaurants, 108 natural hot springs and a swimming pool. The resort is a 50-minute drive from The Wuyi Mountains, a UNESCO World Heritage Site rated for its cultural, scenic, and biodiversity values. All resort rooms are decorated with environmentally-friendly material, reflecting the natural theme of the resort, and giving the space a sense of place.

FOR IMMEDIATE RELEASE

RCI Expands its Global Vacation Offerings with More Than 135 New Resorts in 2017

FOR IMMEDIATE RELEASE

RCI Welcomes 74 Newly Affiliated Properties to its Global Exchange
Network

The affiliated resorts added through the first half of 2017 further strengthens the global presence for the world's leading vacation exchange company.

PARSIPPANY, N.J. (August 15, 2017) – RCI, the global leader in vacation exchange and part of the Wyndham Worldwide family of brands (NYSE: WYN), added 74 new properties to its affiliate exchange network during the first half of 2017. The new affiliations include resorts in Africa, Asia, Europe, India, Latin America, the Caribbean and North America.

"We are excited to welcome these new properties to the RCI® global exchange network," said Gordon Gurnik, president, RCI. "With the addition of these great resorts across sought-after destinations across the globe, we continue to bolster both the number and quality of vacation choices we are able to offer our 3.8 million subscribing members."

In Latin America and the Caribbean, RCI added more than 30 affiliated properties, like the
Sunscape Splash Montego Bay by Unlimited Vacation Club in Montego Bay, Jamaica. Great for a fun-filled getaway made for the whole family, this all-inclusive resort offers travelers access to powdery beaches and features like waterslides, a pirate ship and a lazy river. Parents and kids should enjoy The Explorer's Club, which provides daily programs and supervised fun for young children, and the Core Zone Teen's Club that has special activities and events for teens.

Additionally, RCI subscribing members now have the option to visit Sea Point, South Africa,
Africa, with a stay at the Bantry Bay International Resort. Located a short distance from Cape Town,

these apartments were built against the beautiful backdrop of the sheltered rock-face of the Atlantic Ocean. From each room's balcony, you can enjoy the seemingly endless sea views and listen to the waves hitting the shoreline below.

RCI also saw growth in India with The Ananta Udaipur in Udaipur, Rajasthan, India. Set against the breathtaking backdrop of the Aravalli Hills, the resort is spread across 75 acres of lush greenery, creating a fairy tale-like experience. Contemporary villas and gorgeous amenities coupled with the surrounding picturesque façade offer families a relaxing, luxury experience the area known as the "city of lakes."

In Paphos, Cyprus, the affiliated network welcomed the Royal Blue Hotel and Spa Paphos for subscribing members to enjoy. Situated 700-feet above the coastline, the resort offers panoramic views of Paphos and the surrounding shore. On top of these gorgeous views, world class

The largest vacation exchange network added approximately 80 international properties in 2017 to its global network of over 4,300 affiliated resorts

PARSIPPANY, N.J. (February 21, 2018) – RCI, the global leader in vacation exchange and part of the Wyndham Worldwide family of brands (NYSE: WYN), welcomed more than 135 newly affiliated resorts to its exchange network in 2017. These additions span across every populated continent and feature vacation experiences with great options for nearly every kind of journey, from surf and sun to glittering modern cities.

"Over the past year, we've added some exceptional properties to the RCI® exchange network," said Gordon Gurnik, president, RCI. "Through strategic partnerships with both new and existing affiliates, our 3.8 million subscribing members have thousands of options to choose from in sought-after destinations around the world when planning their next vacation."

In Latin America, RCI added more than 55 resorts, many of which are in notable beach destinations. The Ventus at Marina El Cid Spa & Beach Resort is located in the quaint fishing village of Puerto Morelos, Mexico, along the gorgeous Mayan Rivera. In addition to the beautiful views of the Caribbean Sea, guests can also enjoy the luxurious resort amenities and local cultural experiences from the ancient Mayans that used to inhabit the area.

RCI also enjoyed outstanding growth in the Asia-Pacific region with more than 20 new resorts.
Emerald Terrace Condominium Resort in Phuket, Thailand, is one of the most recent additions. Located on a lush hillside, the resort island is full of tranquil delights and scenic adventures from elephant treks

through the untouched jungle to scuba diving the colorful local playgrounds of marine life.

The company's North American footprint expanded by nearly 50 resorts in 2017 as well. One of these additions includes the Prestige Collection Harbourside at Marker 33 in Indian Rocks Beach, Florida, which offers many family-friendly activities. The resort shares the grounds with Splash Harbour Water Park, and features a 42 foot tall tube slide, single rider body slide, 600 foot relaxing lazy river, extra-large sundeck and zero-entry pool with mushroom waterfalls and ground sprays. The water park also features a splash zone, game room and 18 holes of tropical themed miniature golf.

FOR IMMEDIATE RELEASE

RCI Expands its Global Vacation Offerings with More Than 135 New Resorts in 2017

The largest vacation exchange network added approximately 80 international properties in 2017 to its global network of over 4,300 affiliated resorts

PARSIPPANY, N.J. (February 21, 2018) – RCI, the global leader in vacation exchange and part of the Wyndham Worldwide family of brands (NYSE: WYN), welcomed more than 135 newly affiliated resorts to its exchange network in 2017. These additions span across every populated continent and feature vacation experiences with great options for nearly every kind of journey, from surf and sun to glittering modern cities.

"Over the past year, we've added some exceptional properties to the RCI® exchange network," said Gordon Gurnik, president, RCI. "Through strategic partnerships with both new and existing affiliates, our 3.8 million subscribing members have thousands of options to choose from in sought-after destinations around the world when planning their next vacation."

In Latin America, RCI added more than 55 resorts, many of which are in notable beach destinations. The Ventus at Marina El Cid Spa & Beach Resort is located in the quaint fishing village of Puerto Morelos, Mexico, along the gorgeous Mayan Rivera. In addition to the beautiful views of the Caribbean Sea, guests can also enjoy the luxurious resort amenities and local cultural experiences from the ancient Mayans that used to inhabit the area.

RCI also enjoyed outstanding growth in the Asia-Pacific region with more than 20 new resorts.
Emerald Terrace Condominium Resort in Phuket, Thailand, is one of the most recent additions. Located on a lush hillside, the resort island is full of tranquil delights and scenic adventures from elephant treks through the untouched jungle to scuba diving the colorful local playgrounds of marine life.

The company's North American footprint expanded by nearly 50 resorts in 2017 as well. One of these additions includes the Prestige Collection Harbourside at Marker 33 in Indian Rocks Beach, Florida, which offers many family-friendly activities. The resort shares the grounds with Splash Harbour Water Park, and features a 42 foot tall tube slide, single rider body slide, 600 foot relaxing lazy river, extra-large sundeck and zero-entry pool with mushroom waterfalls and ground sprays. The water park also features a splash zone, game room and 18 holes of tropical themed miniature golf.

ABOUT THE AUTHOR

Allen Kelley has written several books about the Timeshare industry, including "RCI Points User's Guide - Tips, Tricks and Secrets". Other books that he has published include: "The Angel Moroni", and "The Dog that Flew Over 500,000 Miles". He is currently working on a feature length screenplay – " Cowboy Magic", and a TV Pilot – "The Stripe".

Allen has also established a book publishing company called "Dream Magic Productions.

He can be contacted at
dreammagicproductions@gmail.com.

NOTES FOR YOUR NEXT VACATION GO HERE

Your next vacation goes here!

51508110R00066

Made in the USA
Lexington, KY
04 September 2019